HAGAKURE

Hagakure; The Book of Hidden Leaves
ISBN-13: 978-1-937981-41-9

Copyright© 2012 by Mikazuki Publishing House & Hiroki Shima

Author: Hiroki Shima
Illustrator: Hoornaz Mostofizadeh
Publisher: Mikazuki Publishing House
www.MikazukiPublishingHouse.com

Except for use in a review, the reproduction or utilization of this work in any form or by an electronic, mechanical, or other means, now known or hereafter invented, including xerography, photocopying, recording, in any information

storage and retrieval system, is forbidden and prohibited without the written permission of the publisher..

The information contained within this book is for educational and commercial purposes and does not necessarily reflect the views of the publisher.

HAGAKURE

INTRODUCTION

Hagakure is a classic text from the end of the Sengoku Jedai or Warring States period. *Hagakure* is a record of the words of Jyocho Yamamoto Tsunetomo, born on June 11th, 1659 and died in 1719. He lived in a thatched hut in the middle of Mt. Kinryu in the Saga prefecture of Japan. Happily, I was privileged to have many opportunities to learn about the *Hagakure* in my schooldays

HAGAKURE

since my school was located just

about five minutes from this thatched

hut where Yamamoto lived. There are

so many important messages in

Hagakure-Hidden Leaves to enrich

our lives.

My dream was to share a new

and original translation by a Japanese

translator, with the West.   While

some of the content might not sit well

with you, I hope all readers of this

book will grasp some important

HAGAKURE

messages and apply them in their daily life. The original text is very difficult and lengthy. I excerpted some parts and interpreted the meanings. I hope you enjoy this book. Through this book, you can learn the right attitude of servants and the true Samurai spirit. Thanks to my friend Kambiz Mostofizadeh of Mikazuki Publishing House, I could finally have a chance to see this book being published. I also want to use

HAGAKURE

this book as an opportunity to reflect

on myself what I learned from my

junior high teacher.   Jocho

Yamamoto was a retainer of the

Nabeshima Clan and he was versed

in the history of the many hardships of

Lord Naoshige Nabeshima

(1538-1618), Katsushige

Nabeshima (1580-1657), Mitsushige

Nabeshima (1632 – 1700).   While

serving as a retainer living in Saga

Prefecture, he learned many key

HAGAKURE

lessons about how to maintain the

right attitude of a retainer, and the true

Samurai spirit with the focus on the

principle of self-cultivation.

Sincerely,

Hiroki Shima
Author
Hagakure; Book of Hidden Leaves

HAGAKURE

The mindset of the warrior

- ❖ Preparation for death

- ❖ Humble

- ❖ Discontent

- ❖ Compassion

- ❖ Nurture yourself

- ❖ Be ambitious

- ❖ Education

- ❖ Tips of life

HAGAKURE

"The way of the warrior is in Death." The more you become aware of your own mortality, the more you can fulfill your life. So, cherish each moment of your life." We must not have a deep attachment to life. When you wonder whether to live or die, choose death without any hesitation. Compared to living in

HAGAKURE

disgrace, choosing death is wiser.

Live graceful, die beautifully.

The way of the warrior is to prepare

for death anytime.   Know your

mortality.   Our life is just a short

period.   Be prepared to die.

Every morning, calm down

HAGAKURE

your thoughts and consider your last

moment of life. People usually think

that thinking about death is

pessimistic. However, actually,

thinking about death is not a

pessimistic attitude because it makes

you appreciate living.

You should work as a warrior

with all your might.   Try to have the

resolution and determination to die for

HAGAKURE

the sake of your work. If you do so,

even if ten people try to kill you, you

you can beat them.

The resolution of death is an

important mindset. You will be more

aware of your life and cherish your

life.   By looking at the stern reality of

life, you can truly lead your life to one

that is full of satisfaction.

HAGAKURE

You should not fret too much

about minor issues.   Do whatever

you like in life.   Success of a big

project always accompanies with

some minor mistakes.   You shouldn't

worry so much about making minor

mistakes.

HAGAKURE

Again, every morning, calm

down your thoughts. Imagine the days

you would die because of a disaster or

an accident.   Don't let up on yourself.

There is a limit in life.   We

can't live for 150 or 200 years.   Even

if we can prolong our life, it doesn't

HAGAKURE

mean that we can live forever.   From

this reasoning, we should be humble.

Also, we are not living by

ourselves. Thanks to our parents,

teachers, and people around us, we

have been able to live up until today.

When you think about this, we need to

have a humble attitude.

HAGAKURE

HAGAKURE

If you are not sure about

things, ask opinions from others.

Our wisdom is limited.   People will

often make mistakes when they try to

solve everything by themselves.

As we get older, we are likely to

HAGAKURE

preach lessons but people that are

ready to listen to the lessons are rare.

There are much less people who want

to understand the lessons well and

practice. The more we grow, the more

difficult it is to find people to learn

from.

If no one gives you advice, you

will become selfish. Being humble is

the key to success.   If you are

HAGAKURE

humble, you can find many

references.   It's important to have

someone who can advise you.

Be careful what you say and

do.   Keep in mind to talk logically,

with a few words.   A person of few

words is more reliable than talkative

person.

HAGAKURE

Listen carefully to the words of experts.   Even if you know full well about what they are saying, the more you listen to them, you can acquire some special wisdom from them that you had not previously known.

HAGAKURE

Don't be captured by your past manners and customs.   It is impossible to go back to past ages. However, don't put too much value in the modern style.   Those who favor the modern-style and reject the old-style are thoughtless.   The world changes smoothly according to each stage of time.

HAGAKURE

HAGAKURE

Look at the workings of your

mind carefully.   Be honest to yourself.

You should always observe your mind

carefully.   Be careful in your work.

Being humble is the key to

success in everything.   Also, it's

HAGAKURE

important to have an attitude of

discontent. There is no ending point

in our practice. Don't be satisfied in

your practice. If you are satisfied,

you won't progress anymore.

Discontent is the source for us

to improve. Practice every day with

the feeling of discontent. You can go

up to a high stage in life if you take up

this attitude.   By focusing and moving forwarding with determination in gaining expertise, people will look upon you as a specialist.

Don't expect to be regarded as a great person. Just concentrate on your present moment.

HAGAKURE

Our life is the continuation of

each day.   So, when you look back

on the past and re-trace your steps,

you realize how greatly you have

progressed.

Work hard when you are

HAGAKURE

young. Don't boast. Don't lead a

luxurious life. If you don't experience

hardship, you won't be able to nurture

your willpower.

We need to be so strict with

ourselves. When we have

communication with others, we should

have compassion.

HAGAKURE

If water is too clean, fish can't

live.   Likewise, if you are too

scrupulous, people will hate you.

Severe punishment doesn't

work sometimes. When you notice

someone's improper act, try to

overlook their behavior.   Or better

yet, pretend like you didn't see or hear

those behaviors.

Be full of compassion and be

kind to people.   By doing so, you can

build up good relationships with

others.

Present a friendly and

approachable demeanor so that

people will be able to talk with you

easily.

Do not be hesitant to tell your

fault and of your failure.

HAGAKURE

It is not necessary to point out

your friends' mistakes.   They will

realize their mistakes on their own.

Praise good points of people

and encourage them.

HAGAKURE

HAGAKURE

Try to make a harmonious

relationship with others so that you

can correct their mistakes and

cooperate.

Use kind words to your

subordinate.   Benefit other people as

HAGAKURE

much as you can.

Nurture a simple and sturdy

spirit.   By doing so every day, you

can win against enemies no matter

when they attack you.

Train yourself to a level that no

HAGAKURE

one can beat you.

Among all people around you,

you should aim to be the best person

at all times.   Otherwise, you can't win

against the enemy.

Servants should have a

HAGAKURE

competitive spirit.   Work hard until

you harbor a conceited mind.   Once

you have that mind, you should

dispel other minds and just focus on

your work genuinely.

Having good friends are

important.   Keep away from bad

friends, and try to have many good

friends.   By doing so, you can

HAGAKURE

cultivate your mind by encouraging

each other.   Especially if you are over

30, you find it harder and harder to

find people who would correct your

mistakes.   Without being aware of

your mistakes, you are likely to

behave selfishly.   So, you need to

find people who could enlighten you

wherever you are.

Don't miss your chance.   Be

HAGAKURE

determined and do not stop until you

reach your objectives.

Quick decision-making is

important.   It is no use worrying

about things too much. Finish the task

promptly.   Too much consideration is

of no use.   Calm down and breathe

seven times.   Then judge things

immediately.

HAGAKURE

In one view, planning ahead is important. Think of the future plan carefully. Then properly you can plan. For example, if you make an appointment with an important person, try to see what kind of person he would be. What do they enjoy or dislike? Try to make an effort to have a harmonious relationship with others.

HAGAKURE

Be confident in life. Don't

hesitate in everything. Be

courageous. Too much worrying is

not good. Be confident in what you

do and what you say. Your dream

will come true easily.

HAGAKURE

HAGAKURE

Don't be so nervous about making

mistakes.   Be pleased with your

troubles.   When you try to

accomplish some big enterprise, don't

care so much about minor mistakes.

When you encounter troubles, try to

think that this is a good opportunity to

improve yourself.   Once you

overcome this situation, you can go

towards the next step.   Polish your

ability.   Make your effort so that no

one can reach your level.   Even if you

make mistakes, people don't care so

much about your mistakes as you

think.

Be prepared for losing jobs in

your lifetime.   If you are well

prepared for losing jobs, even if you

HAGAKURE

lose your job, it will be ok.   Too much

worry is meaningless.

Even if you are still not yet

successful in your workplace, don't

worry about it.   If a person

progresses very quickly, people

around him will become an enemy.   If

you are very slow in progressing your

career, people will still help you and

HAGAKURE

much more happiness will come to

you.

If you are a supervisor, you

should lead your subordinates with

compassion.

Even if a person's growth is

slow, be patient and educate them.

HAGAKURE

If you are kind and tolerant, they will gradually open up their mind and they will try to improve.

The Four Types of Retainers

❖ Speedy worker

❖ Bit speedy worker

❖ Bit slow worker

❖ Slow worker

Speedy worker

Receives a order or command from his master and completes the job quickly.

HAGAKURE

Bit speedy worker

Receives a job but the

response is slow.   However, the job is

completed once the job is started.

Bit slow worker

Upon receiving the job, the

response is prompt.   However, the

completion of the job is somewhat

slow.

Slow worker

Upon receiving the task, the

response is slow. Not only that, the

completion of the task is slow.

Overall, most of the people are "Bit

slow workers" and "Slow workers."

It's important to educate people

to learn the history of our own

province.   History is the story full of

endeavors and hardships of our

ancestors.   If you learn in detail,

naturally you will be motivated to

HAGAKURE

admire ancestors.   You would feel

the gratitude for your ancestors.   If

everyone feels gratitude for their

ancestors, then morals would

improve.   So, learning the history is

the essence to stabilize our society.

Four vows

❖ Don't get behind in the way of
   the warrior

❖ Serve your master

❖ Be dutiful to your parents

❖ Benefit other people

Keep in mind these four vows. These

HAGAKURE

four vows will create the proper

mindset. If you memorize these

phrases and put them into practice,

you won't be led astray from the way

of the warrior.

"Don't go behind in the way of the

warrior" meaning to practice your skill

and be brave in everything.

"Serve your master" meaning that as

a servant, you should admonish your

master and give stability to your

organization.

HAGAKURE

"Be dutiful to your parents" meaning that you should give respect and filial duty to your parents.   Serve your master wholeheartedly and respect your parents.

"Benefit other people" meaning that you should have a large amount of compassion and that you should raise masters and useful people.

*If you try to complete these four vows, you can proceed on your path step by step.

Wear modest clothes. People judge your ability from your appearance. If you were wearing a expensive clothes, then people will take it for granted that you do an excellent job. If you wear modest clothes, people will regard you as a mediocre person. So when you do an excellent job, people will surprise

and praise you a lot. Expensive

clothes put you at a disadvantage

because if you make some mistake,

people will look down on you.

When you are invited to a

wonderful place, you should feel so

grateful to be invited instead of

thinking how uncomfortable it is to

have to go.

HAGAKURE

When your acquaintance gets

sick, try to talk positive words to them

when you visit.   If you talk about

negative things, they will feel

depressed.

Don't judge things based on selfish
motives.

HAGAKURE

To govern the society is not a big

issue.   Just follow what I said until

now.   Your country would become

truly peaceful.

In order to relax your mind, put

a little spit on your earlobe & breathe

deeply.   You can calm yourself down.

HAGAKURE

NOTES

(Please use this page for comments)

HAGAKURE

NOTES

(Please use this page for comments)

HAGAKURE

NOTES

(Please use this page for comments)

HAGAKURE

NOTES

(Please use this page for comments)

HAGAKURE

NOTES
(Please use this page for comments)

HAGAKURE

NOTES
(Please use this page for comments)

HAGAKURE

MIKAZUKI PUBLISHING HOUSE TITLES
Swords & Sails; The Legacy of the Red Lion

The Medium Writer; Unshattered Spirits

Palloncino; The Arrival of Palloncino

The Card Party

Tokiwa; A Japanese Love Story

Arctic Black Gold

The Bribe Vibe

Find the Ideal Husband

I Dream in Haiku

Stories of a Street Performer

The Adventures of Jasper

MMA Coloring Book

HAGAKURE

Mage Magnus

Fortune Cookie Politics

John Locke's 2nd Treatise on Civil Government

Learning Magic

Mikazuki Jujitsu Manual

Magic as Science & Religion

Karate 360

25 Principles of Martial Arts

Letting the Customers Win

Political Advertising Manual

Mikazuki Political Science Manual

Small Arms & Deep Pockets

HAGAKURE

World War Water

More Titles Coming Soon
Visit www.MikazukiPublishingHouse.com

for more information on our books.

Mikazuki Publishing House is a book

publishing house specializing in a variety of

fiction, non-fiction, and Childrens books.

Press Contacts interested in arranging press

interviews and/or author appearances, are

welcome to contact:

pr@MikazukiPublishingHouse.com

HAGAKURE

三日月

"EDUCATION IS THE KEY TO HAPPINESS"

www.ingramcontent.com/pod-product-compliance
Lightning Source LLC
Chambersburg PA
CBHW031613040426
42452CB00006B/496